Wicked
IRISH

BY HOWARD TOMB
Illustrations by Jared Lee

WORKMAN PUBLISHING • NEW YORK

ACKNOWLEDGMENTS

Many thanks to Ward Calhoun for his imagination, the
M. Storans of Croom for their crucial help and hospitality, Seosamh McCloskey and Barra Ó Donnabháin for
their translation and Sally Kovalchick and Patty Brown
for their skill and patience.

Library of Congress Cataloging-in-Publication Data
Tomb, Howard, 1959–
  Wicked Irish for the traveler / by Howard Tomb.
    p. cm.
  ISBN 0-7611-1355-X (alk. paper)
  1. Irish language—Conversation and phrase books—Humor.
2. Ireland—Description and travel—Humor. I. Title.
PN6231.I7T66 1999
491.6'283421'0207—dc21   98-45821
                        CIP

Workman books are available at special discounts when purchased in
bulk for premiums and sales promotions as well as for fund-raising or
educational use. Special editions or book excerpts can also be created
to specification. For details, contact the Special Sales director at the
address below.

Workman Publishing Company
708 Broadway
New York, NY 10003-9555

Manufactured in the United States of America
First Printing June 1999
10 9 8 7 6 5 4 3 2

CONTENTS

SOCIAL IRELAND

SIGHTSEEING AND OTHER THRILLS

SEVERAL DOZEN WELCOMES

You could enjoy Ireland without Irish, the native tongue. You could also enjoy a slice of bread without slathering it with fresh butter and marmalade. But life is short and vacations are shorter. If you want something easy and predictable, visit England.

The English imposed their language on Ireland, Scotland and Wales, and they weren't terribly nice about it. The roots of Irish managed to survive in the rocky soil, however.

In Ireland, Irish is also called "Gaelic." It's widely spoken in the Gaeltacht, or Irish-speaking areas, which you'll find in the west.

You'll hear Irish in the streets, on the radio and, as you try to learn it, in your nightmares.

Yes, you may find it difficult to pronounce and impossible to understand, but the Irish warmth is legendary; any effort you make to speak the language will be welcomed. Go ahead and *bain triail as* (try it). At worst, you'll bring a little more laughter into Irish life.

PRONUNCIATION

While English invaders failed to destroy the Gaelic language, they did isolate it for long periods of time, so today it sounds different depending on where it's spoken. The pronunciation in this book is meant to emulate Munster Irish, which they speak in exquisite towns such as Dingle, Sneem and Skibbereen.

Wherever it's spoken, Gaelic sounds like a combination of Swedish and Hebrew. In other words, you haven't the slightest chance of pronouncing it well by relying on this book alone.

Two sounds can't be faked: the gargled "g"— *gh* in the pronunciation column—and the glottal "ghkgh" you find in the German "achtung" and Scottish "loch," which makes you sound like you're trying to dislodge a fish bone from the back of your throat. We'll denote it with *kh*.

The alien collections of letters the Irish call "words" make pronunciation look harder than it is. To get over your fear of the written language, repeat the following phrases on the left while staring at their Irish translations on the right.

Teddy O'Kennedy	**Teidí Ó Cinnéide**
telephone	teileafón
plan	plean
leprechaun	leipreachán
poteen	poitín
banshee	bean sí

DISCLAIMER

Due to the unpredictable course of Irish events, including but not limited to weather and associated visibility or lack thereof, the sudden appearance of domestic animals or stone-deaf old gents in Wellingtons, standing or prone, in the road or in public accommodations, and owing to the cumulative impact of stouts, bitters, whiskeys, lagers, berry syrups, jet lag and puddings black and white, the author and his publisher, editors, translators, agents, publicists, lawyers, accountants, personal trainers, armed response security team and crazed guard dogs hereby reject, pummel into the turf and dance on the heads of any and all claims or actions that may arise from the use, misuse or disuse of this volume or its many sister volumes, or any of the words, phrases or concepts herein. God bless.

CELTIC CUSTOMS

Irish authorities object to the importation of weapons, narcotics and certain forms of information, such as written descriptions and photographs of naked people. Should you encounter customs agents upon your arrival, keep up the chatter and you'll breeze right through.

I have nothing to declare.	*Níl rud ar bith le hadmháil agam.*	*NEEL rud air BIH leh had-VAWL uh-GUM.*
You won't want to open this bag.	*Ní bheifeá ag iarraidh an mála so a oscailt.*	*Nee VEH-faw eg EE-uh-rig un MAW-luh suh uh OS-gilt.*
It took me half an hour to shut the damn thing.	*Thóg sé leathuair orm an rud damanta a dhúnadh.*	*HOAG shay LAH-oor OR-um uhn ROOD DAH-muhn-tuh uh GHOO-nuh.*
Jesus, Mary and Joseph!	*'Íosa, 'Mhuire's a Iósaif!*	*EES-uh, VWIR-us uh YOA-sif!*
'Tis a grand machine gun you have there, officer!	*Togha meaisínghunna atá ansan agat, a dhuine uasail!*	*TAU-uh mah-SHEEN-ghun-uh uh-TAW un-SUN uh-GUT, uh GHWIN-uh OO-uh-sil.*

TAXING CABBIES

To hail a taxi in Ireland, you'll need to make a phone call or walk to a taxi stand. (Petrol is so expensive that hacks don't cruise the streets looking for fares.) Many drivers will be happy to explain points of interest during the ride.

I beg your pardon?	*Gabhaim pardún agat?*	*GAH-vim pahr-DOON uh-GUT?*
What?	*Cad é?*	*KAHD EH?*
You may as well speak Irish.	*Bheadh sé chomh maith agat Gaoluinn a labhairt.*	*VAY-ukh shay khoa MAH uh-GUT GWAY-lin ALLOW-irht.*
I can't understand a word of your English.	*Ní thuigim focal Béarla uait.*	*Nee HIH-gim FO-kuhl BAYR-luh wit.*

IRISH ROAD KILL

If you feel you must rent a car, ask a lot of questions and make your wishes clear at the rental agency before you sign anything. Keep in mind that some credit card companies refuse to grant the usual complementary insurance coverage to cardholders foolish enough to rent cars in Ireland.

Insurance? Hell yes!	*Árachas? Ba mhaith liom, ambaist!*	*AW-ruh-khuhs? Buh VAH lyom, am-BASHT!*
Give me all you've got.	*Tabhair dom a bhfuil le fáil de.*	*TOOR dom uh VWIL leh FAWL deh.*
Does that include long-term disability?	*An bhfuil míchumas fadtéarmach clúdaithe?*	*Uh VWIL mee-KHUM-us fahd-TAYR-mukh KLOO-duh-huh?*
What about death and dismemberment?	*Cad fé bhás agus sracadh coirp?*	*KAHD fay VAWS UH-gus SRAHK-uh KORP?*
Does the car come with airbags/head-stones?	*An dtagann an carr le haermhálaí/leaca tuama?*	*Uh DAHG-un un KAHR leh hayr-VAW-lee/LAHK-uh TOO-uh-muh?*

DRIVING TIPS

Safe driving depends on good habits and instincts, since you don't have time to think in emergencies. That's why life is so dangerous on the left side of the road: the habits you've nurtured for as long as you've been driving are suddenly wrong. A simple right turn could be murder.

Irish cars have standard transmissions, so you have to drive *and* shift on the left. Most roads feature potholes and stone walls (known as "ditches" or "hedges"), not shoulders. Where you'd expect an intersection you'll find a round-about. The urge to drink can be powerful (What's an Irish vacation without alcohol, after all?), but impaired drivers go home in a box.

DO NOT

▶ Drive at night
▶ Drink and drive
▶ Attempt to become airborne on bumpy roads
▶ Transport livestock without permission

DO

▶ Grab every last scrap of insurance
▶ Rent the largest car you can find to gain a New-tonian advantage in a head-on collision
▶ Ask the rental agent for religious statuary
▶ Consider a bus tour

ON GUARD

The *gardái,* or Irish police, watch the roads for Yanks, who are known as uniquely idiotic drivers who drive too slowly, take left turns too sharply, grip the steering wheel too tightly and, of course, drive on the wrong side of the road.

I didn't mean to drive on the right.	*Ní rabhas ag tiomáint ar an taobh deas d'aon turas.*	*Nee RAUV-us eg tih-MAWNT ayr uh TAYV DASS dayn TUR-uhs.*
But we call it the "right" side because it's right.	*Ach tugaimíd an "taobh deas" air mar tá sé go deas.*	*Ahkh TUG-a-meed un TAYV DASS ayr mahr TAW shay go DASS.*
The back seat of your cruiser is rather cramped.	*Tá suíchán cúil do chruiser saghas cúng.*	*TAW see-KHAWN kool do KHROO-zur sais KOONG.*
Haven't you people ever heard of a Chevy Caprice?	*Nár chuala sibh riamh trácht ar Chevy Caprice?*	*Nawr KHOO-uh-luh shiv REE-uhv TRAWKHT ayr Chevy Caprice?*

ROAD SIGNS

Before getting behind the wheel, familiarize yourself with Ireland's unique road signs.

YET ANOTHER BEEHIVE HUT

TWEED NEXT 100 MILES

PLAINTIVE PENNY WHISTLE NEXT LEFT

NOW ENTERING DEEP REMORSE

TOUGH GOLF AHEAD

SLOW NUN

BIG FAMILY CROSSING

FINDING YOUR WAY

As you explore Ireland, you'll see ancient hills, magnificent ruins, thousands of miles of handmade stone walls and several million bewildered sheep—over and over and over again. Since they all look the same, you'll undoubtedly become lost. Unfortunately, the Irish, when giving instructions, aren't any more direct than their roads.

Excuse me, lass/lad.	*Gabh mo leithscéal, a chailín/leaid.*	*GUH mo lesh-GAYL, uh kha-LEEN/LAD.*
Is this the way to the Dripsey?	*An é seo an bealach ceart go dtí an Druipseach?*	*UHN YAY shuh un BAH-lukh KYART go DEE un DRIP-shukh?*

🧳 TRAVEL AND ACCOMMODATION

Aha. Do *not* turn left after one mile.	*Há, ná cas ar chlé tar éis míle slí.*	*Hah, NAW kahs ayr KHLAY tar AYSH MEE-luh SHLEE.*
I should *not* bear right at the church.	*Níor chóir dom druidim chun deisil ag an séipéal.*	*NEER khoar dom DRID-im khun DESH-il ag uh SHAY-payl.*
If I go straight I'll miss it.	*Má théim go díreach ar aghaidh, raghad thairis.*	*Maw HAYM guh DEE-rukh ayr AIG, RAI-uhd HAR-ish.*
Grand. Now I know how *not* to go.	*Go hiontach. Tá 'fhios agam anois conas gan dul ann.*	*Guh HOON-tukh. TAW iss uh-GUM uh-NISH KUN-us GAN dul aun.*
Luckily, I'm *not* in a rush.	*Tá an t-ádh liom ná fuil deabhadh orm.*	*TAW un TAW lyom NAW fwil DYAU-uh ur-um.*

MASTER THE ROAD WAVE

The farther you drive from urban centers, the more you'll be expected to wave to the drivers of oncoming cars. Waving your arm or hand, however, would make people think you were either a spastic comedian or a Brit. The correct Irish road wave engages a driver's index finger only, which is raised from the top of the steering wheel in a split-second jig.

To calculate the proper extension of your finger, use the formula where d is the distance from Galway in miles, v is the combined velocity of the vehicles in miles per hour, p is the population of the nearest town, and μ is your hangover rated on a scale of 1 to 10, where 10 feels like your frontal lobe is a moth-eaten Aran sweater.

$$\frac{1024(d)^2}{v(p)\mu}$$

WHEN IRISH EYES ARE PRYING

Anyone with a sofa bed can
offer "bed and breakfast."
Use a few discouraging
words if things get
too personal.

We adore the thatched roof/low ceiling.	*Is breá linn an ceann tuí/ tsíleáil íseal.*	*Iss BRAW lin un KYAUN TWEE/ tee-LAWL EE-shul.*
Please remove the straw from my hair.	*Bain an sop féir óm ghruaig/ shúil, le do thoil.*	*BWIN un sop FAYRh oam GHROO-igleh duh HIL.*
Your children are delightful, mum.	*Tá do pháistí gleoite, a bhean uasal.*	*TAW duh PAWSH-dee GLOA-tyuh, uh VAN OO-uh-sul.*
Kindly get them out of our room.	*Ar mhiste leat iad a ruaigeadh amach as ár seomra.*	*Ur VISH-dih lat EE-uhd uh ROO-uh-gyuh uh-MAKH as awr SHOAM-ruh.*
My wife and I would like to make some of our own.	*Ba mhaith liom agus mo bhean tabhairt fé chúpla díobh a dhéanamh dár gcuid féin.*	*Buh VAH lyom UH-gus mo VAN TOORHT fay KHOOP-luh deev uh YAY-nuv dawr gwid FAYN.*

SLIGHTLY BEYOND MURPHY'S BED

Before William Murphy introduced the Murphy bed, which folds up into a wall or closet, people couldn't walk into a typical Dublin hotel room without getting footprints on the bed. The wise traveler inspects the accommodations before relinquishing the plastic.

How did you get the bed in here?	*Conas ar éirigh libh an leaba a thabhairt isteach?*	*KUH-nus ur AI-rhig liv un LAH-buh uh HOORHT ish-DYAKH?*
What a charming 18th-century bathroom/ blanket/TV!	*M'anam go bhfuil sé go hálainn mar sheomra folctha/ phlaincéad/ theilifíseán ón ochtú haois déag!*	*MAH-num go VWIL shay go HAW-lun mahr HYOHM-ruh FOLK-huh/flan-KAYD/hell-ih-fee-SHAWN oan OKH-too HEESH dayg!*
Hmm. Hot water is 50 pence a minute?	*Hmm. Uisce te ar chaoga pingin an nóiméad?*	*Hmm. ISH-gih teh ayr KHWAY-guh PING-uhn un NOH-mayd?*

💼 *TRAVEL AND ACCOMMODATION*

That would explain the manly smell on the bus.	*Tuigim anois an boladh fearúil ar an mbus.*	*TIG-im uh-NISH un BOL-uh far-OOL ayr un MUSS.*
Could you recommend something roomier/more upscale?	*Arbh fhéidir leat rud éigin níos fairsinge/ galánta a mholadh?*	*Ur-uv AY-dir lyat rood AY-gin nees FAHR-shing-uh/guh-LAWN-tuh uh VOL-uh?*
Say, a decent park bench?	*Binse deas sa pháirc, abair?*	*BIN-shuh DASS suh FAWRK, AH-bur?*

YOUTH HOSTILE

You don't have to be young to take advantage of the youth hostels all over Ireland. But if you want to get any sleep, you may need eyeshades, a pair of earplugs and a stern demeanor.

You're in my bunk.	*'S é sin mo bhuncsa.*	*SHAY SHIN muh VUNK-suh.*
See these stains?	*An bhfeiceann tú na smálacha so?*	*Uh VEK-un too nuh SMAWL-ukh-uh suh?*

🧳 TRAVEL AND ACCOMMODATION

They're mine.	*Mo chinn féin atá iontu.*	*Muh heen FAYN uh-taw IN-tuh.*
Now turn off the bloody light.	*Múch an diabhal solas anois.*	*MOOKH un DYAU-ul SOL-lus uh-NISH.*
And shet the feck up.	*Agus dún do focan clab.*	*UH-gus DOON duh FOK-un klab.*

TRAVELER'S PRAYER

Hey, St. Jude, patron saint of lost causes, I beg you to forgive us our mockery of this gloomy weather and grant us just a single afternoon that's only partly cloudy, Your Holiness. Let the locust-like plague of rain move east to fall on the English and their Protestant trees and let one or two rays of sun shine down from on high to remind us that there is a loving God in heaven who would smile on Ireland and our vacation, if only long enough for us to dry our socks, Your Divinity. And hey, if you get a chance, take a sad song and make it better.

A WEE BIT OF HISTORY

8000 B.C.: Mistaking Irish Channel for heavy fog, Scottish shepherds wander into Ireland. They miss their sheep and go home, but memory lingers for hours.

3000 B.C.: Druids get lost in fog. They hug rocks and trees, sleep late, fail to bathe.

A.D. 432: St. Patrick arrives with literature, persuades pagan Celts to stop praying to rocks and trees. Convinces snakes they can swim. Invents green beer.

c. 600–795: Golden Age: *Book of Kells,* first dirty limericks, etc.

795: Vikings, off to rape and pillage in England, lose their way in the fog and invade Dublin. Spend next 200 years raping and pillaging Ireland.

1014: Brian Boru, "Emperor of the Irish," under cover of fog, whips Vikings. They move to Minnesota.

1171: Strongbow from England invades and plays factions off each other. Under cover of fog, crowns himself king.

1171–present: Brits try to hang on. Under cover of fog, Irish earls flee. Chaos, rebellion, treachery, murder, poetry remain.

CULTURE

1845: Microbes, under cover of fog, attack potato plants. Remarkably, weather stays wet for years. Microbes thrive, causing Great Famine. A million die; another million join the NYPD.

1904: Bloomsday, June 16, subject of Joyce's *Ulysses.* Anyone claiming to have read the whole book is full of blarney.

1916: Rebels proclaim Irish Republic, surrender and die. Liam Neeson wins starring role.

1920: Britain divides north and south. The Irish decide in a referendum that instead of slasher films, they will have national politics.

1922: Free State established. North left out. IRA convention.

1969– present: British troops in North. Bombs, bullets, bullets, bombs, ceasefire, bombs, bombs, bullets, ceasefire, bombs, bullets, bombs, ceasefire.

1990s: Rise of "Gaelic Tiger" and offspring, "Gaelic Yuppies." Tony Ryan builds hotels, buys Jackie O's biggest diamond. Bono, Doyle and surviving McCourts get rich.

PORTRAIT OF THE TOURIST AS A YOUNG LITERATURE MAJOR

Ireland produced some of the twentieth century's greatest writers in the English language, most of whom left the country as soon as they could borrow enough money to buy a pair of shoes. To understand their work—and gain insight into the Irish character—consider how the greats would have said, "There's a sheep."

Swift: I cannot tell a ewe from ram
But know for sure it be no ham.

Yeats: Her haunches and her four black feet
Cause my red-rose heart to beat.

Shaw: Aha! Is that General Beard at his dinner?

Joyce: Me sees a white swelling in the crotch o' the valley!

Beckett: I see nothing. Wool, perhaps. Perhaps not. No.

GAELO-MATIC QUICK REFERENCE GUIDE

More smoked salmon.	*Tuilleadh bradáin deataithe.*	*TWIL-uh BRAH-dawn DATA-huh.*
No mutton, thank you.	*Diabhal caoireoil, go raibh maith agat.*	*DYAU-ul KWEE-roal, guh rev MAH uh-GUT.*
Another round.	*Babhta eile.*	*BAU-tuh EL-uh.*
To your health.	*Fé thuairim do shláinte.*	*Fay HOO-uh-rim duh HLAWN-tuh.*
To the Pope's health.	*Fé thuairim sláinte an Phápa.*	*Fay HOO-uh-rim SLAWN-tuh un FAW-puh.*
To your dog's health.	*Fé thuairim sláinte do mhadra.*	*Fay HOO-uh-rim SLAWN-tuh duh VAH-druh.*
Help!	*Fóir orm!*	*FOARH ur-um!*
I've fallen and I can't get up.	*Thiteas agus ní féidir liom éirí.*	*HIT-us UH-gus nee FAY-dir lyom AI-ree.*

LASH 'EM, THRASH 'EM

To keep warm the Irish play a lot of sports that require running around and shouting. These include hurling (the game, not the reverse peristalsis), Gaelic football, sheep dog trials and horse racing, where betting quickens the pulse and lightens the wallet.
Join the fun with these
all-purpose cheers.

Hey, twinkle-toes!	*Hóigh! A chleiteoigín!*	*HOA-ig! Uh khleht-oag-EEN!*
Get on your bike, boyo!	*Suas ar do rothar, a mhic!*	*SOO-us ayr duh RUH-hur, uh vick!*
Everyone knows your mother!	*Tá aithne ag an saol mór ar do mháthair-se!*	*TAW AH-nyuh eg uh SAYL MOAR ayr duh VAW-hir-shuh!*
And not for her cooking!	*Agus ní mar gheall ar a cuid cócaireachta!*	*UH-gus NEE mar YAWL ayr uh KWID KOAK-uh-rukh-tuh!*

LET'S TALK SHEEP

Any cow that survives the Irish weather tends to tumble down the steep hills into the ocean. That's why sheep are so popular in Ireland: they have heavy coats and do not roll very far. When you meet a shepherd, start a conversation by sharing your keen observations.

Hey, those are sheep, right?	*Dheara, caoirigh atá iontu san, nach ea?*	*YEH-ruh, KWEE-rig uh-TAW in-tuh sun, nakh AH?*
These sheep are soooooooo cute!	*Nach gleoooite atáid!*	*Nakh GLOOAA-tuh uh-TAWD!*
They look like they're wearing little wool sweaters!	*Cheapfá go raibh geansaithe beaga olla orthu!*	*HYAP-faw guh rev GAN-suh-huh BYUG-uh UH-luh or-huh!*
Which one is your favorite?	*Cé acu ceann is ansa leat?*	*KYUH-kuh KYAUN is AN-suh LAT?*
She's lovely indeed.	*Tá sí go hálainn, muise.*	*TAW shee go HAW-lun, MUSH-uh.*
Do you prefer the leg or the chop?	*An fearr leat an chos nó an gríscín?*	*Un FAR lat un KHOS noa un GREESH-keen?*

CULTURE

SLUR O'RAMA

The Irish will almost certainly treat you with patience and kindness, but should you become seriously impaired by alcohol and decide to insult someone, here are some pungent phrases. Be sure to have a getaway vehicle at the curb and a stunt driver at the wheel.

collie breath	*a bhodmhadra*	*uh VOD-VAD-ruh*
organ meat	*a bhodaigh*	*uh VOD-ig*
summer teeth*	*a mhantacháin*	*uh VAN-tuh-khawn*
spud nut	*a mhagairlí prátaí*	*uh VAH-gur-lee praw-TEE*
crafty leprechaun	*a lúracháin lúbaigh*	*uh loo-ruh-KHAWN LOO-big*
sot-snorkel	*a shoic gaimse*	*uh hok GAM-shuh*

* some are there,
  some aren't

📖 **CULTURE**

UNRAVELING A YARN

In Ireland, even the smallest transactions can become social events. No matter how long the line at the supermarket is, for example, the cashier may exchange pleasantries and news with each customer in turn. You might speed things up with a couple of polite remarks that they will understand and respect.

Excuse me, lassies.	*Gabhaim pardún agaibh, a chailíní.*	*GAH-vim par-DOON uh-GWIV, uh KHAIL-een-ee.*
Couldn't you wind it up?	*Nárbh fhéidir libh críoch a chur leis sin?*	*NAW-ruv AY-dir liv KREEKH uh chur lesh shin?*
I'm late for the wake.	*Táim mall don dtórramh.*	*TAWM MALL don DOA-ruv.*
No, I don't know who died.	*Níl, níl a fhios agam cé fuair bás.*	*NEEL, NEEL iss uh-GUM KAY FOO-ir BAWS.*
But I want to get there before the liquor's gone.	*Ach ba mhaith liom a bheith ann sara mbeidh an deoch ar fad imithe.*	*AKH buh VA lyom uh veh A SAH-ruh ME un DYOKH a fad IH-mih-h*

CULTURE

DIAL A SAINT

Where you find Catholic scholars and martyrs, there you find saints. When the time comes for prayer in Ireland, it may help to know where to direct your petition.

SAINT	CLAIM TO FAME	DAY	CURRENT SPECIALTY
Anthony (c. 251–356)	leading hermit	1/17	finding lost luggage
Brendan (c. 486–578)	discovered America	5/16	catching a flight home
Brigid (452–523)	turned water into beer	2/1	instant happy hour
Cecilia	survived beheading	11/22	song requests; neck pain
Columba (521–597)	raised the dead	6/9	surviving a hangover
Luke (1st century A.D.)	early "doctor"	5/1	surviving Irish medical care
Mary (c. 22 B.C.– c. A.D. 40)	bore son of God, moved to Ireland	8/15	explaining an unexpected pregnancy
Patrick (c. 415–492)	converted the pagans	3/17	patron saint of U.S. party animals

OUR FATHER KNOWS BEST

If you must confess in Ireland, the local father will help you seek forgiveness—particularly if you make a donation, treat him at the pub and make an effort to use Gaelic.

Forgive me, Father, for I have sinned.	*Beannaigh mé, a Athair, mar is peacach mé.*	*BAN-ig may, uh AH-hir, mahr is PACK-ukh may.*
It's been three pints/days/years since I last confessed.	*Tá trí phiont/ lá/bliana ann ó dheineas faoistin.*	*TAW TREE FYONT/LAW/ BLEE-uh-nuh aun oa YIN-us FWEESH-din.*
I insulted/ groped/the guests/clergy/ deceased.	*Mhaslaíos/ ghlámas ar ma haíonna/ sagairt/mairbh.*	*Vas-LEES/ GHLAW-mus ayr nuh HEE- nuh/SAH- girt/MAH-riv.*
Six Hail Marys and ten pounds in the box?	*Fáilte an Aingil fé shé agus deich bpunt sa bhosca?*	*FAWL-tuh un AHNG-il fay HAY UH-gus DEH BOONT suh VOS-kuh?*
Thank you, Father!	*Go raibh maith agat, a Athair!*	*Guh rev MAH uh- GUT, uh AH-hir!*
Might I buy you a beer?	*Arbh fhéidir liom beoir a cheannach duit?*	*Ur-uv AY-dir lyom BYOAR uh HYAN-nukh dit?*

CULTURE 📖

GENUFLECT LIKE YOU MEAN IT

If you're not Catholic but get dragged into church by your local lover to repent what you did on Saturday night, you'll want to learn to genuflect.

Before sitting in a pew, get down on your right knee (or at least bend your knees, ye of little fitness). The lower you bend, and the harder time you have getting up, the greater the effect. To lay it on extra-thick, bow your head.

Using your right hand, touch your "head, crotch, wallet and watch." Or, in more polite terms, forehead, sternum, left nipple and right nipple.*

When you get up to leave the pew, repeat the procedure before you turn your back to the altar. If you can do it all nonchalantly, no one has to know you're headed straight to hell.

*Note: Never use the words "crotch" or "nipple" in church, and do not express your concern that Jesus' dainty loin-cloth might fall off.

SURVIVING A PADDY'S BREAKFAST

The full Irish breakfast—cereal, juice, bread, butter, jam, eggs, sausage, bacon and blood pudding—was invented by people who worked hard outdoors for up to sixteen hours a day in all kinds of weather. They had to eat huge amounts of high-calorie foods in order to die young and get some rest. Today they equate hospitality with animal fat.

The sausage/ pudding looks lovely, indeed.	*Tá cuma bhreá ar an ispín/ bputóg, muis.*	*TAW KUM-uh VRAW ayr un ish-PEEN/buh-TOAG, MUSH.*
Sadly, I must decline.	*Ní feidir liom, faraoir.*	*Nee FAY-dir lyom, fah-REER.*
I've given up pig entrails/ congealed blood for Lent.	*D'éiríos as ionathar muice/ fuil théachtaithe le haghaidh an Charghais.*	*Dai-REES as IH-nuh-hur MWICK-uh/FWIL HAYKH-tuh-huh leh HAIG an KHAR-eesh.*
Lucky you! Our Lent runs through Christmas!	*Ortsa an t-ádh! Leanann ár gCarghas féin go dtí an Nollaig!*	*ORT-suh un TAW! LAH-nun awr GAR-ees FAYN guh DEE un NOL-ig!*
Just one more scone would thrill/kill me.	*Ba bhás dom/ bhreá liom bonnóg amháin eile.*	*Buh VAWS dom/ VRAW lyom bon-OAG uh-VAWN EH-luh.*

FIVE EASY PIECES OF ICE

The Irish have plenty of tea, and they have ice, but they do not have iced tea. They love new ideas, so go right ahead and explain the concept to them.

I'd like iced tea.	*Ba mhaith liom tae oighrithe.*	*Buh VAH lyom TAY AI-rih-huh.*
Yes, it's a complex formula.	*Sea, meanglam casta atá ann.*	*SHAH, MANG-glum KAS-tuh uh-TAW AUN.*
Do you feel your brain cramping up?	*An mothaíonn tú t'inchinn ag crapadh agat?*	*UH mo-HEEN too TIN-hin uh KRAP-uh uh-GUT?*
Just bring me a glass of ice and a pot of tea.	*Tabhair dom gloine leac oighir agus pota tae, agus sin é é.*	*TOORH dom GLIN-uh LAK AI-irh UH-gus POT-uh TAY, UH-gus shin AY AY.*
I'll take over from there.	*Réiteod féin an chuid eile de.*	*Ray-TYOAD FAYN un KHWID ELL-uh deh.*

SPUD WITH A THOUSAND FACES

Every country has a food or drink that can bring tears to
your eyes. France has burgundy. Italy has olive oil. And
Ireland has potatoes. People eating Irish potatoes have
the same look on their faces as babies at the
breast. At mealtime, don't
hold back.

I'll start with roasted potatoes.	*Tosnód le prátaí rósta.*	Tos-NOAD leh PRAW-tee ROAS-tuh.
For my salad, boiled potatoes.	*Prátaí beirithe mar shailéad dom.*	PRAW-tee BER-ih-huh mar hah-LAYD dom.
I'll take a side of fried potatoes.	*Beidh sceallóga prátaí agam ar leataoibh.*	BEG shkawl-LOAG-uh PRAW-tee uh-GUM ayr lah-TEEV.
The mashed potato entree.	*Brúitín prátaí mar phríomh-chúrsa.*	Broo-TEEN PRAW-tee mar FREEV-KHOOR-suh.
And for dessert, the spud pudding.	*Agus mar iarphroinn, an mharóg phrátaí.*	UH-gus mar EE-ur-frin, un vah-ROAG FRAW-tee.

LAST CRAWL FOR ALCOHOL

If you were to travel the length and breadth of Ireland sampling all the varieties of whiskey, you'd be as dead as Brendan Behan. The very name of the spirit is said to come from *uisce beatha,* or "water of life." It's easy to make friends with the fish who swim in that water.

What're you drinkin', fella?	*Cad tánn tú ag ól, a bhuachaill?*	*KAD TAWN Too eg OAL, uh VOO-uh-khil?*
I'll have what he's having.	*Beidh agamsa atá aigesean.*	*Beg uh-GUM-suh uh-TAW EG-uh-shun.*
Ack Ack! Mother Mary!	*Aic! Aic! A Mháthair Mhuire!*	*Ack! Ack! Uh VWIR-uh VAW-hir!*
That goes down like a nun's knickers.	*Téann san síos ar nós fobhríste mná rialta.*	*TAYN sun SHEES ayr NOAS fo-VREESH-di MNAW REE-ul-tuh.*
I pray it comes up easier.	*Guím go dtaga sé aníos níos éasca.*	*GWEEM go DAG-uh shay uh-NEES nees AYS-guh.*

✕ *FOOD, DRINK AND RECOVERY*

SHARE THEIR PAIN

Irish history contains little but suffering, separation, longing and poetry. You can hear it all set to music in the pubs, where each song is more melancholy than the next.

The music is wonderful.	*Tá an ceol go hiontach.*	*TAWN KYOAL guh HOON-tukh*
I haven't cried like this since I was two.	*Níor chaoineas mar so ó bhíos dhá bhliain d'aois.*	*NEER KHWEEN-us mar SO oa VEES ghaw VLEE-un DEESH.*
I felt cheerful when I came in here.	*Bhíos gealgháireach ar theacht isteach dom.*	*VEES gyal-GHAWR-uch ayr HAKHT ish-DAKH dom.*
Now I'm planning my own wake.	*Táim ag pleanáil mo thórraimh féinig anois.*	*TAWM uh plan-AWL mo HOA-riv FAYN-ig uh-NISH.*
Bartender! More Paddy's!	*A fhear a' tí! Tuilleadh Paddy's!*	*Uh AR uh TEE! TWIL-luh Paddy's!*

WHISKEY FLAVOR WHEEL

The aficionado of Irish whiskey has different tastes from, say, the cabernet lover. Where the effete wine expert salivates for hints of berries and flowers, the tough, uncompromising whiskey drinker prizes the taste of pickled fish and diesel fumes. Whiskey fans use a flavor wheel like this one to categorize, describe and rank their favorite poisons. Use these terms to join in spirited discussions at the bar.

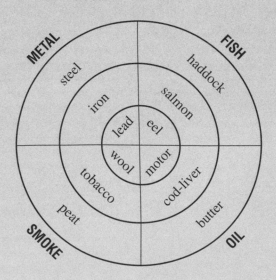

METAL

FISH

steel
iron
haddock
salmon
lead
eel
wool
motor
tobacco
cod-liver
peat
butter

SMOKE

OIL

✕ FOOD, DRINK AND RECOVERY

ENGLISH	IRISH	PRONUNCIATION
METAL	**MIOTAL**	*MIH-tul*
steel	**cruach**	*KROO-ukh*
iron	**iarann**	*EE-uh-run*
lead	**luaidhe**	*LOO-uh-yuh*
FISH	**IASC**	*EE-usk*
haddock	**cadóg**	*kah-DOAG*
salmon	**bradán**	*bruh-DAWN*
eel	**easconn**	*ASS-gun*
SMOKE	**DEATACH**	*DAH-tukh*
wool	**olann**	*UH-lun*
tobacco	**tobac**	*tuh-BAK*
peat	**móin**	*moan*
OIL	**OLA**	*UH-luh*
motor	**mótar**	*MOA-tur*
cod-liver	**ae troisc**	*ay TRUSHK*
butter	**im**	*im*

FOOD, DRINK AND RECOVERY ✗

ANGELA'S WARPATH

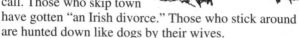

Certain Irishmen fail to
show up for dinner on
payday and forget to
call. Those who skip town
have gotten "an Irish divorce." Those who stick around
are hunted down like dogs by their wives.

What does he look like again?	*Cén sórt dealraimh atá air arís?*	*Kayn SORT DYAL-riv uh-TAW ayr uh-REESH?*
Was he carrying a wad of cash?	*An raibh lab mór airgid aige?*	*Uh REV LAB moar AH-ruh-gid EG-uh?*
Is he the kind of guy who sings and buys rounds for everybody?	*An é an saghas duine a bhíonn ag canadh agus ag ceannach deochanna do gach aon duine?*	*Un AY un SAIS DIN-uh VEEN uh KAH-nuh UH-gus uh KYAN-nukh DYOKH-un-na do GAKH AYN DIN-uh?*
No, I can't say that I've seen him.	*Ní dóigh liom go bhfaca mé é.*	*Nee DOA-ig lyom guh VA-kuh may ay.*
Not when he's bought me three pints.	*Go háirithe agus trí phiont ceannaithe aige dom.*	*Guh HAW-rih-huh UH-gus tree FYONT KYAN-nih-huh EG-uh dom.*

POOL 'N' DART NIGHT

Billiards and darts are more than pastimes in Ireland; they're national obsessions. The only chance at beating the locals at their own games is to spoil their concentration.

Mother Mary, you've a dainty touch!	*A Mhuire Mháthair, tá lámh bhanúil agat!*	*VWIR-uh Uh VAW-hir, TAW LAWV van-OOIL uh-GUT!*
I'm surprised you missed that shot.	*Is ionadh liom gur theip an iarracht san ort.*	*Iss OO-nuh lyom gur HEP un EE-uh-rukht san ort.*
I love your shoes. They're hilarious.	*Is breá liom do bhróga. Táid scléipeach ar fad.*	*Iss BRAW lyom duh VROA-guh. TAWD SHKLAY-pukh ayr fad.*
I hear the women in this town are easy to know.	*Cloisim go mbíonn mná an bhaile seo ana-ghrámhar.*	*KLISH-im guh MEEN MNAW uhn VAH-lih shuh AH-nuh GHRAW-vur.*
Got any sisters?	*Aon deirfiúracha agat?*	*AYN dayr-ih-FOOR-uch-uh uh-GUT?*

CLOSE ENCOUNTERS OF THE PUB KIND

Irish blokes who've drunk their way out of work receive their "dole," or welfare money, on the same day of each month. Then, like dying salmon, they surge into the pubs that day to convert every last "punt" into ethanol. Should you happen upon such a scene on "Dole Day," gain favor with soothing compliments and any help you can offer.

I love your nose.	*Is breá liom do shrón, muise.*	*Iss BRAW lyom do HROAN, MUSH-uh.*
I am astonished by its size/ color/veins/ craters.	*Cuireann a méid/dath/ féitheoga/ cráitéir ionadh an domhain orm.*	*KIR-un uh MAYD/DAH/fay-HYOA-guh/kraw-TAYR OO-nuh an DAUN OR-um.*
Your jowls/ guts are also impressive.	*Téann do gheolbhacha/ bholg i bhfeidhm orm chomh maith.*	*TAYN duh YOAL-vukh-uh/VOL-ug ih VAIM OR-um khoa MAH.*
Are you able to walk?	*An bhfuil tú in ann siúl?*	*Uh VWIL-too in aun SHOOL?*
Could I offer you a ride home/ coronary surgery?	*An bhféadfainn síob abhaile/ obráid chroí a thairiscint duit?*	*Uh VAY-tin SHEEB uh-VAL-ih/uh-BRAWD KHREE uh HARH-ish-kint dit?*

📷 *SIGHTSEEING AND OTHER THRILLS*

QUIVERDANCE

Although you may never develop a taste for Irish dancing, you ought to be a good enough guest to find some pleasant things to say about it.

They put up quite a racket, now, don't they?	*Ambaist tá raic cheart á tógaint acu, ná fuil?*	*Am-BASHT taw RACK HYART aw TOAG-int a-kuh, naw FWIL?*
They sweat all over the place.	*Táid ag cur allais ar fud na háite.*	*TAWD uh cur AWL-ish ayr fuhd nuh HAW-tuh.*
I must say it looks familiar.	*Tá seana-chuma air seo, caithfead a rá.*	*Taw SHAN-uh-KHUM-uh ayr SHUH, KAH-hud uh RAW.*
That's how we kill roaches in New York City.	*Is mar sin a mharaímíd ciaróga dubha i Nua Eabhrac.*	*Iss mar SHIN uh vah-ree-MEED kee-uh-ROA-guh DOOV-uh ih NOO-uh OW-ruk.*

DETECTING THE SIGHTS OF DUBLIN

Joyce called Dublin the Center of Paralysis. Use these lines
if you'd like to be more diplomatic.

Isn't it a lovely town you have here!	*Nach deas an baile mór atá anso agaibh!*	NAKH DASS un BAH-lih MOAR uh-TAW un-SUH uh-GWIV!
A park with trees and grass!	*Páirc a bhfuil crainn is féar inti!*	PAWRK uh VWIL KREEN is FAYR IN-tih!
Right in the city! Imagine!	*Sa chathair féin! Samhlaigh é!*	Suh KHA-hir FAYN! SAU-lig ay!
And the marvelous bridges that go all the way across the river!	*Agus na droichid iontacha a théann an bealach ar fad trasna na habhann!*	UH-gus nuh DRIH-hid OON-tuh-khuh uh HAYN un BAL-ukh ayr fad TRAS-nuh nuh HOW-un!
More's the pity.	*Is mór an trua é.*	ISS MOAR un TROO-uh ay.
I must catch the next train to anywhere.	*Caithfead imeacht ar an gcéad traein eile go háit ar bith.*	KAH-hud IM-ukht ayr uh gayd TRAYN EL-uh guh HAWT ayr bih.

DUBLIN ON FIVE PINTS AN HOUR

Dublin has clean streets, little crime and 900 pubs. In other words, it may be the best place to get faced in all of Europe. In *Ulysses,* James Joyce immortalized the joys of staggering around Dublin. Here's how to continue the tradition.

I'm trying to follow in Leopold Bloom's footsteps.	*Táim ag iarraidh céimeanna Leopold Bloom a leanúint.*	*TAWM eg EE-uh-rig KAY-muh-nuh Leopold Bloom uh lah-NOONT.*
I keep getting lost.	*Téim ar strae arís agus arís eile.*	*TAYM ayr STRAY uh-REESH UH-gus uh-REESH EL-uh.*
Could you direct me to Davy Byrne's pub/ Bella Cohen's brothel?	*Arbh fhéidir leat mé a stiúradh i dtreo thigh tábhairne Davy Byrne/drúthlann Bella Cohen?*	*Ur-uv AY-dir lyat may uh SHTOO-ruh ih DROA HIG TAU-ur-nuh Davy Byrne/DROO-lun Bella Cohen?*
Could I kiss you/ stand you a pint?	*Arbh fhéidir liom póg a thabhairt/piont a cheannach duit?*	*Ur-uv AY-dir lyom POAG uh HOORHT/ PYONT uh HYAN-nukh dit?*
Yes I said yes I will yes.	*Sea a dúrt, sea, sea.*	*SHAH uh DOORT, SHAH, shah.*

THE ILLUMINATED DOODLE

When in Dublin, thrill to the 1200-year-old illuminated Gospels known as the *Book of Kells,* and its many sister bibles, at Trinity College. No matter what your religion, you're sure to find something to talk about in the ancient monk's wild illustrations.

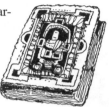

I'm curious about these drawings.	*Táim fiosrach fé na líníochtaí seo.*	*TAWM FIS-rukh fay nuh LEE-nee-ukh-tee shuh.*
These seem far ahead of their time.	*Tá cuma roimh a n-aimsir ar fad orthu.*	*TAW KUM-uh riv uh NAM-shirh ayr FAD or-huh.*
This style didn't reappear until the early Grateful Dead posters.	*Níor tháinig an stíl seo ar an saol arís go dtí moch-phóstaeirí na Grateful Dead.*	*Neer HAW-nig un SHTEEL sho ayr un SAYL uh-REESH guh DEE MOKH-foas-TAYRH-ee nuh Grateful Dead.*
What kind of ol-Aid were y serving in monastery teria?	*Cén saghas Lucazade a bhíodar a riar i bproinnteach na mainistreach?*	*KAYN SAIS LOO-kuh-zayd uh VEE-dur uh REE-ur ih BRIN-takh nuh MAN-ish-trukh?*

STOUT-BELLIED MEN

According to the Law of Frozen Daiquiris, the better-tasting the drink, the quicker it goes down. If you plan to spend, say, five hours in a row drinking with friendly people, you must take precautions if you want to be able to get out of bed the following afternoon.

First, defend your stomach. Coat it with viscous substances that can withstand the solvents you will ingest. Mashed potatoes and Irish stew suit this purpose perfectly. Half a loaf of dense brown bread can serve as a buffer to prevent sudden assaults on the central nervous system.

Visitors who wish to remain upright should not try to match the locals' pace. Remember: *THEY HAVE TRAINED FOR THIS EVENT FOR GENERATIONS.*

When your turn comes, you must order your drinking partners another round. But your salvation will come from *declining a refill for yourself* and nursing the remainder of your drink. That way, your partners will "lap" you and order you another drink just when they finish the ones you bought for them.

Using this method, you will consume considerably less alcohol than the locals (and spend less money). According to Gringo's Law, you will be twice as drunk as they are, but someone is sure to help you stagger home.

SHOP 'TIL YOU STOP

Only the most confused shopper
would cross the Atlantic Ocean
to buy Irish goods, which are
widely available in the United
States. Your careful browsing,
on the other hand, can help a salesperson pass the time—
at absolutely no cost to you!

What handsome china/crystal/ linen/sheep-related products!	*Ná fuil an deilf/criostal/ lín/na táirgí caora-cheangailte slachtmhar!*	*NAW FWIL un DEL-if/KRIS-tul/LEEN/nuh TAWR-ih-gee KWAY-ruh-HANG-il-dih SLAKHT-vur!*
Do you have that in a different color/ pattern/size?	*An bhfuil a leithéid sin agaibh i ndath/ bpatrún/dtomhas eile?*	*Uh VWIL uh leh-HAYD shin uh-GWIV ih NAH/bah-TROON/DAU-us EL-uh?*
Please show me everything you have in stock.	*Taispeáin dom a bhfuil agaibh sa tsiopa, le do thoil.*	*Tash-BAWN dom uh VWIL uh-GWIV suh TYOP-uh, leh duh HIL.*

📷 SIGHTSEEING AND OTHER THRILLS

No, nothing today, thank you.	*Faic dom inniu, go raibh maith agat.*	*FAK dom in-NYUHV, guh rev MAH uh-GUT.*
I'll get it cheaper at Macy's.	*Gheobhainn níos saoire é ag Macy's.*	*YOA-in nees SEE-ruh ay eg Macy's.*

TESTING IRISH HOSPITALITY

While you wait to "cash up" at the automated teller machine, take the opportunity to meet the friendly natives in line.

Ireland is more expensive than I expected.	*Tá Éire níos costasaí ná mar a bhíos ag súil leis.*	*TAW AYRH-uh nees KOS-tuh-see naw mar uh VEES uh SOOL lesh.*
Can you believe it?	*An féidir leat é a chreidiúint?*	*Un FAY-dir lat ay uh hreh-DOONT?*
I'm down to my last punt.	*Níl ach punt fágtha agam.*	*Neel akh POONT FAWG-huh uh-GUM.*
Is it true the Irish are generous hosts?	*An fíor gur óstaigh fhlaithiúla iad na hÉireannaigh?*	*Un FEER gur OAS-dig lah-HOOL-uh EE-ud nuh HAYRH-uh-nig?*
Be a good man/woman and lend me your cash card.	*Tabhair iasacht do chárta airgid dom, mar a dhéanfadh fear maith/bean mhaith.*	*TOORH EE-uh-sukht duh KHAWR-tuh AR-uh-gid dom, MAR uh YAYN-ukh FAR MAH/BAN VAH.*

EXPLORING THE ROYAL RUBBLE

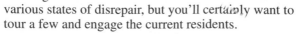

Irish castles and churches often appear together, since people tend to fight for religious reasons. These buildings lie in various states of disrepair, but you'll certainly want to tour a few and engage the current residents.

Did your forebears live in this building?	*An raibh cónaí ar do shinsir romhat san áras so?*	*Uh rev KOAN-ee ayr duh HIN-shir ROA-ut sun AWR-us suh?*
When did it last have a roof?	*Cathain cheana a bhí díon air?*	*KAH-hin HAN-uh uh VEE DEEN ayr?*
Are you planning any renovations?	*An bhfuil tú ag smaoineadh ar athóiriú ar bith?*	*Un VWL too uh SMWEEN-uh ayr AH-KHOA-rhoo ayr bih?*
Do you think the prince/princess had any teeth?	*An dóigh leat go raibh aon fhiacla ag an bprionsa/ mbanphrionsa?*	*Un DOA-ig lyat guh REV AYN EE-uh-kluh eg uh BRIN-suh/MAN-frin-suh?*

THE SHAM'S ROCK

According to legend, you can get "the gift of gab" at Blarney Castle in County Cork. Lean over a hundred-foot drop and swap spit with a rock that's been kissed by millions of tourists who ate bacon for breakfast. Your charm will quadruple and flowery phrases will roll off your tongue.

You're lovely as a meadow/ Druid/nun in May.	*Tá tú chomh hálainn le móinéar/Draoi/ bean rialta i mí na Bealtaine.*	*TAW too KHOA HAW-lun leh moa-NAYR/ DREE/BAN REE- ul-tuh ih MEE nuh BAL-tin-uh.*
Your voice is like a song/ foghorn/ cabbage.	*Tá do ghuth cosúil le ceol/bonnán ceo/cabáiste.*	*TAW duh GHUH ko-SOOL leh KYOAL/bun- AWN KYOA/kuh- BAWSH-dih.*
Where you walk, there spring a thousand flowers/leaks.	*San áit a siúlann tú, eascraíonn míle bláth/fuarán.*	*Sun AWT uh SHOOL-un too, ass-KREEN MEEL-uh BLAW/ foo-uh-RAWN.*
The day you were born, angels wept tears of joy/ grief/Guinness.	*An lá a rugadh thú, shil na haingil deora áthais/bróin/ Guinness.*	*Un LAW uh RUG- ukh hoo, HILL nuh HANG-gil DYOAR-uh AW- hush/BROAN/ Guinness.*

BETTER LEFT UNSAID

In order to avoid misunderstandings and hurt feelings, use the proper terms for everyday items and activities.

Irish English	Irish Gaelic	Pronunciation	American English
jelly	*glóthach*	*GLOA-hukh*	Jell-O, candy
chips	*sceallóga*	*shkawl-OAG-uh*	French fries
jacket	*craiceann*	*CRACK-un*	potato skin
knacker	*cladhaire*	*KLAI-uh-ruh*	bum, loser
knickers	*fobhríste*	*foh-VREESH-dih*	underwear
jackeens†	*jeaicíní*	*jack-EEN-ee*	Dubliners
culchies‡	*cábóga*	*kaw-BOAG-uh*	rednecks
shell suit*	*culaith allais*	*KULL-ee AWL-ish*	sweatsuit
top o' the mornin'*	*mora dhuit*	*MOR-uh gwit*	howdy, pardner!
go for a ride‡	*dul ag marcaíocht*	*DULL uh MARK-ee-ukht*	have sex

† slightly rude
‡ extremely rude
* subject to severe ridicule

LINKS ON THE BRINK

Some say the Vikings invaded Ireland primarily to get decent tee times. The equipment has changed since then, but the scores haven't, and neither has the weather. Impress your caddy with your determination and command of Gaelic—if not your game

Is this weather typical?	*An mbíonn an aimsir mar seo de ghnáth?*	*Uh MEEN un AM-shih mar shuh deh GHNAW?*
I'm not accustomed to 12-foot breakers in a water hazard.	*Níl cleachtadh agam ar thonnta dhá throigh déag ar airde i bhfiontar uisce.*	*Neel KLAKH-tuh uh-GUM ayr HUN-tuh GHAW HRIH DYAYG ayr AR-dih ih VIN-tur ISH-guh.*
Are the ruins/fairy forts out of bounds?	*An bhfuil na fothracha/ liosanna thar teorainn?*	*Uh VWIL nuh FOH-rukh-uh/LISS-un-na har TOA-rin.*

📷 SIGHTSEEING AND OTHER THRILLS

Should I replace divots in consecrated ground?	*Ar chóir dom scraithíní a chur thar nais i dtalamh coisricthe?*	*Ur KHOAR dom skrah-HEEN-ee uh khur har nash ih DAL-uv KOSH-rik-huh?*
It's a tricky lie.	*Is luí casta é.*	*Iss LEE KAS-duh ay.*
Am I entitled to relief from this dolmen/ewe/ leprechaun?	*An bhfuil faoiseamh ag dul dom ón dolmain/gcaora/ lúrachán so?*	*Uh VWIL FWEE-shuv uh gul dom oan DOL-uh-min/GWAY-ruh/loo-ruh-KHAWN so?*
Shite! I don't usually lose a putt in the wind.	*Cacamas! De ghnáth ní chaillím amas sa ghaoth.*	*KAH-kuh-mus! Deh GHNAW nee KHA-leem AH-mus suh GHWAY.*

YOUR TURF ACCOUNTANT

Gambling is an honored and legal form of entertainment in Ireland. A licensed bookie, known as a "turf accountant," will take bets from you, the "punter," on almost any-thing—from the Irish Sweepstakes to the price of mutton. Thanks to the luck of the Irish, he'll usually win.

When is the next race/ election?	*Cathain a bheidh an chéad rás/ toghchán eile ann?*	*KAH-hin uh VEG un HAYD RAWS/tau-KHAWN EL-uh aun?*
I like the mare from Kentucky/ widow from Donegal.	*Is maith liom an láir ó Kentucky/ an bhaintreach ó Dhún na nGall.*	*Iss MAH lyom un LAWR oa Kentucky/un VAN-trukh oa DHOON nung ALL.*
Who's on the Riviera this weekend?	*Cé tá ar an Riviera an deireadh seachtaine seo?*	*KAY TAW ayr uh Riviera un DEHR-uh SHAKH-tin-uh shuh?*
I'll bet two pounds the paparazzi catch Prince Charles topless.	*Cuirfead dhá phunt go n-aimseoidh na paparazzi an Prionsa Séarlas bráid nocht.*	*KUR-hud GHAW FOONT guh NAM-shoa-ig nuh paparazzi un PRIN-suh SHAYR-lus BRAWD NUKHT.*

YOUR VERY EXTENDED FAMILY

When in Ireland, grab a local phone book and start calling people with your surname. Although the Irish are baffled by our search for "roots," some will invite you over for a cuppa. You might even cadge a free meal.

Hello! I'm visiting from the United States.	*Haló! Táim ar cuairt osna Stáit Aontaithe.*	*Huh-LOA! TAWM ayr KOO-irt OS-nuh STAWT AYN-tuh-huh.*
Yes, I'll be right over.	*Maith go leor, beidh mé ann láithreach.*	*MAH guh loar, BEG may aun LAW-rukh.*
You look exactly like my uncle/ aunt/cousin.	*Tá tú ana-dhealraitheach lem uncail/ aintín/chol ceathair.*	*TAW too AN-uh YAL-rih-hukh lem UNK-il/an-TEEN/KHOL KYAH-hir.*
He/she is a millionaire/ convicted sex offender.	*Is milliúnaí/ ciontóir gnéis é/í.*	*ISS mil-YOON-ee/KYON-toar GNAYSH ay/ee.*
Say, do I smell corned beef and cabbage?	*Cogar, an iad mairteoil shaillte agus cabáiste a bholaím?*	*KOG-ur, un EE-ud mar-TYOAL HAL-tih UH-gus kuh-BAWSH-dih uh vol-EEM?*

POLITICS, RELIGION AND HEALTH

The locals will want your views on important topics of the day and will happily share their opinions with you, particularly late in the evening at the pub. But when the talk turns to politics, sin or papal infallibility, keep your thoughts to yourself.

Lord save us!	*Go sábhála Dia sinn!*	*Guh saw-VAW-luh DEE-uh shin!*
Isn't that a fascinating argument/ lecture/sermon?	*Nach argóint/léacht/ seanmóir le dealramh san?*	*Nakh AR-uh-goant/LAYKHT/ SHAN-uh-MOAR leh DAL-ruv sun?*
I'm out of my depth on that one.	*Tá san ró-dhoimhin domsa.*	*TAW san roa-GHAIN DOM-suh.*
You're a genius/windbag/ loon.	*Is Arastatail ceart/gaotaire/ gealt thú.*	*Iss AH-ruh-stah-til KYART/ GWAY-tuh-ruh/GYALT hoo.*
Why haven't they put you in charge/a straight jacket?	*Cén fáth nár cuireadh tú i gceannas/ jeaicead teann?*	*Kayn FAW nawr KWIR-ukh too ih GYAN-us/JACK-ud TYAWN?*

KISS MY APHORISM

Irish, being a rich and ancient language, includes vast offerings of blessings and curses. Choose one phrase from each column to create your own aphorisms. Begin with a line from column A, add a line from B, and conclude with a line from C.

A	B	C
may the road **Go n-éirí** *Guh NAI-rhee*	rise to meet **an bóthar** *un BOA-hur*	your face **i t'aghaidh** *ih-TAIG*
may the wind **Go séide** *Guh SHAY-dih*	flow through **an ghaoth** *un GHWAY*	your teeth **trí t'fhiacla** *tree TEE-uh-kluh*
may the pudding **Go raibh** *Guh REV*	always be on **an phutóg** *un foot-TOAG*	your Sunday best **i gcónaí ar do chulaith Dhomhnaigh** *ih goa-NEE ayr duh KHOOL-ee GOWN-ig*
may the sun **Go dtaitní** *Guh DAH-nee*	shine on **an ghrian** *un YREE-un*	your worst enemy **ar do namhaid is measa** *ayr duh NAU-id iss MASS-uh*
may the fairies **Go dtóga** *Guh DOAG-uh*	take **na púcaí** *nuh POO-kee*	your livestock **do bheithígh** *duh veh-HEEG*

ROMANCING A LASSIE

Traditional Irish
women are said to
recognize only two
forms of romantic
love: adoration and
pregnancy. Modify
your lines according
to the route you want
to take.

You're the most brilliant/nurturing person I've ever met.	*Is tusa an duine is aibí/cothaithí a casadh riamh orm.*	*Iss TOOH-suh un DIN-nuh iss ABBY/KOH-huh-hee uh KAS-ukh REE-uv or-um.*
Your ankles are like jewels/granite.	*Is mar sheoda/eibhear do rúitíní.*	*Iss mar HYOA-duh/EV-ur duh roo-TEEN-ee.*
I admire the beauty/convenience of your breasts.	*Is aoibhinn liom scéimh/caothúlacht do chíocha.*	*Iss EE-vin lyom SHKAYV/KWAY-hool-ukht duh HEEKH-uh.*
But I'm spellbound by your eyes/deltoids.	*Ach táim fé dhraíocht ag do shúile/deltoids.*	*Akh TWM fay GHREE-ukht eg duh HOOL-yuh/deltoids.*

ROMANCING A LADDIE

Many an Irishman sets his mother on a pedestal, and why not? Anyone who survives a dozen childbirths has earned her sainthood. Because no other woman will live up to that ideal, you must *appear* to share his devotion to the most important woman in his life.

There's nowhere I'd rather live than in your hometown.	*B'fhearr liom bheith i mo chónaí i do bhaile dúchais ná in aon áit eile.*	*BAR lyom VEH ih muh khoa-NEE ih duh VAH-luh DOO-khush NAW in AYN AWT EL-uh.*
Across the street from your dear sweet mum.	*Trasna an bhóthair ód mhamaí ionúin.*	*TRAS-nuh un VOA-hir oad vah-MEE ih-NOON.*
I'd weed her garden every Saturday.	*Bhainfinn na fiailí sa ghairdín di gach Satharn.*	*VIN-hin nuh FEE-uh-lee suh ghar-DEEN dee gakh SAH-hurn.*
Eat her stew every Sunday.	*D'íosfainn a stobhach gach Domhnach.*	*DEES-hin uh STAU-ukh gakh DAU-nukh.*
And kiss her arse 'til doomsday.	*Agus phógfainn a tóin go lá an Luain.*	*UH-gus FOAK-inn uh TOAN guh LAW un LOO-in.*

IN LOVING MEMORY

Oppression, famine and war have allowed the Irish to
forge a special relationship with death; funerals are par-
ties, at least for the more distant relatives. No matter how
you're related, offer up affection as part of your condo-
lence (as well as to earn your pints).

I understand she/he wielded a sharp wit.	*Tuigim gur duine gasta a bhí inti/ann.*	*TIG-im gur DIN-uh GAS-duh uh vee IN-tih/AUN.*
Unmatched as a mother/ father/ brawler.	*Ní raibh a m(h)acasamhail* de mháthair/ athair/amhas ann.*	*Nee REV uh M(V)AK-uh-sau-il deh VAW-hir/AH-hir/AU-us AUN.*
A mighty hurler/singer.	*Iománaí/ amhránaí gaisciúil.*	*Ih-MAW-nee/au-RAW-nee GASH-kyool.*
Deeply devout/ kind/old.	*Fíor-chráifeach/ chineálta/aosta.*	*FEER KHRAW-fukh/hin-NAWL-tuh/AYS-duh.*
And a great one for the drink!	*Agus duine mór óil!*	*UH-gus DIN-uh MOAR OAL!*
Can I get you something from the bar?	*Arbh fhéidir liom rud éigin a fháil duit ón mbeár?*	*Ur-uv AY-dir lyom rud AY-gin uh AWL dit oan MAWR?*

*Use *macasamhail* for women, *mhacasamhail* for men.

THE INEVITABLE THANK-YOU NOTE

Experienced travelers write a thank-you note to everyone they meet on a trip. This improves international understanding and their chances of getting free food and lodging on a return visit. Writing your notes in Gaelic will add a special luster to your sentiments.

You were kind to put me up for the night/ weekend/ summer.	*Bhí sé go deas uait lóistín a thabhairt dom don tseachtain/ deireadh seachtaine/ tsamhradh.*
I've never had a warmer welcome.	*Níor cuireadh fáilte chomh mór san romham riamh.*
I loved the food/ conversation/ kids/animals.	*B'aoibhinn liom an bia/an comhrá/na páistí/na hainmhithe.*
I'm glad you didn't ask me to shovel manure before breakfast.	*Tá áthas orm nár iarr tú orm an bualtach a ghluaisteáil roimh bhricfeast.*

SOCIAL IRELAND

I'll never forget the smell of your barn/ sweater/peat fire.	*Ní dhéanfad dearmhad go deo ar bholadh do sciobóil/ gheansaithe/ thine mhóna.*
I've done some more genealogical research.	*Tá tuilleadh taighde ghinealaigh déanta agam.*
It turns out we're not related after all!	*Tarlaíonn sé ná fuil gaol eadrainn tar éis an tsaoil!*
A rotten shame!	*Mo léan géar!*
Yours truly,	*Is mise le meas,*